T0394874

TOP 10 MOMENTS IN SOCCER

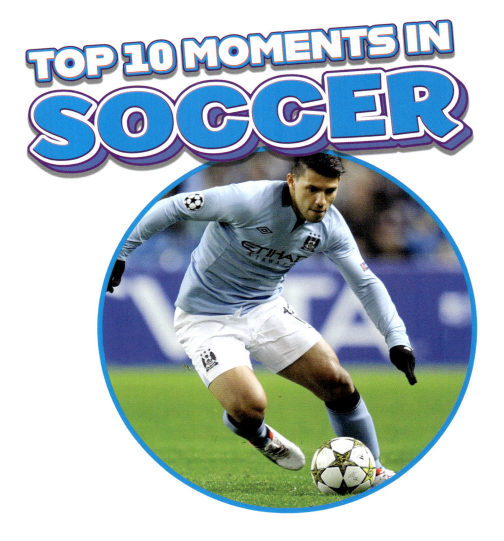

BY NATHAN SOMMER

Minneapolis, Minnesota

Credits

Cover and title page, © Clint Hughes/Associated Press and © fotokitas/Adobe Stock and © pixfly/Adobe Stock; 4, © SergejsKuznecovs/Adobe Stock and © Cristina Villar Martin/Adobe Stock and © L.F.otography/Adobe Stock and © Zoran Obradovic/Adobe Stock and © drazen__zigic/Adobe Stock and © Gorodenkoff/Adobe Stock and © Yuri Arcurs/peopleimages.com/Adobe Stock and © P.Dziurman/Adobe Stock and © master1305/Adobe Stock and © matimix/Adobe Stock and © Alphaspirit/Adobe Stock and © gorynvd/Adobe Stock and © Jacob Lund/Adobe Stock and © T and emBr and ing/Adobe Stock and © Joe/Adobe Stock and © 103tnn/Adobe Stock and © coachwood/Adobe Stock and © Michael Stifter/Adobe Stock and © Sergey Nivens/Adobe Stock and © Lightfield Studios/Adobe Stock and © Allistair F/peopleimages.com/Adobe Stock and © kovop58/Adobe Stock and © Jim Cox/Adobe Stock and © Sergey Nivens/Adobe Stock and © Africa Studio/Adobe Stock and © Philip/Adobe Stock; 5, © Jamie McDonald/Getty Images; 6, © PA Images/Alamy Stock Photo; 6–7, © Thomas Kienzle/Associated Press; 8, © Robert Cianflone/Getty Images; 8–9, © Robert Cianflone/Getty Images; 10, © Robert Michael/AFP/Getty Images; 10–11, © Robert Michael/AFP/Getty Images; 12, © Luis Gene/AFP/Getty Images; 13, © Mike Egerton/EMPICS/Getty Images; 14–15, © Johannes Eisele/Getty Images; 15, © ODD and ERSEN/Getty Images; 16–17, © James Williamson – AMA/Getty Images; 17, © Dan Mullan/Getty Images; 18, © Bettmann/Getty Images; 18–19, © Popperfoto/Getty Images; 20, © Paul Bereswill/Getty Images; 20–21, © Staff/AFP/Getty Images; 22TR, © PA Images/Alamy Stock Photo; 22ML, © Icon Sport/Getty Images; 22BR, © Laurence Griffiths/Getty Images; 23BR, © grey/Adobe Stock

Bearport Publishing Company Product Development Team

Publisher: Jen Jenson; Director of Product Development: Spencer Brinker; Editorial Director: Allison Juda; Editor: Cole Nelson; Editor: Tiana Tran; Production Editor: Naomi Reich; Art Director: Kim Jones; Designer: Kayla Eggert; Designer: Steve Scheluchin; Production Specialist: Owen Hamlin

Statement on Usage of Generative Artificial Intelligence

Bearport Publishing remains committed to publishing high-quality nonfiction books. Therefore, we restrict the use of generative AI to ensure accuracy of all text and visual components pertaining to a book's subject. See BearportPublishing.com for details.

Library of Congress Cataloging-in-Publication Data

Names: Sommer, Nathan, author.
Title: Top 10 moments in soccer / by Nathan Sommer.
Other titles: Top ten moments in soccer
Description: Minneapolis, Minnesota : Bearport Publishing Company, 2026. |
   Series: Top 10 sports extremes | Includes bibliographical references and
   index.
Identifiers: LCCN 2025001546 (print) | LCCN 2025001547 (ebook) | ISBN
   9798895770665 (library binding) | ISBN 9798895775134 (paperback) | ISBN
   9798895771839 (ebook)
Subjects: LCSH: Soccer--History--Juvenile literature.
Classification: LCC GV943.25 .S659 2025 (print) | LCC GV943.25 (ebook) |
   DDC 796.334--dc23/eng/20250213
LC record available at https://lccn.loc.gov/2025001546
LC ebook record available at https://lccn.loc.gov/2025001547

Copyright © 2026 Bearport Publishing Company. All rights reserved. No part of this publication may be reproduced in whole or in part, stored in any retrieval system, or transmitted in any form or by any means, electronic, mechanical, photocopying, recording, or otherwise, without written permission from the publisher. Bearport Publishing is a division of FlutterBee Education Group.

For more information, write to Bearport Publishing, 3500 American Blvd W, Suite 150, Bloomington, MN 55431.

CONTENTS

The World's Sport 4

#10 Rapinoe's Olimpico 5

#9 The Miracle of Istanbul 6

#8 Going Undefeated 8

#7 The Header Heard 'Round the World 10

#6 Messi's Solo Goal 12

#5 Saving the Day 13

#4 Kicking for Gold 14

#3 2022 World Cup Final 16

#2 Pelé Bursts onto the Scene 18

#1 The Goal of the Century 20

Even More Extreme Soccer Moments 22

Glossary 23

Index 24

Read More 24

Learn More Online 24

About the Author 24

THE WORLD'S SPORT

Soccer is the most-watched professional sport in the world. Fans from all around the globe come together to enjoy its fast-paced action, fierce **rivalries**, and extreme plays.

WHAT ARE THE TOP 10 MOMENTS IN SOCCER?

Read on to decide for yourself. . . .

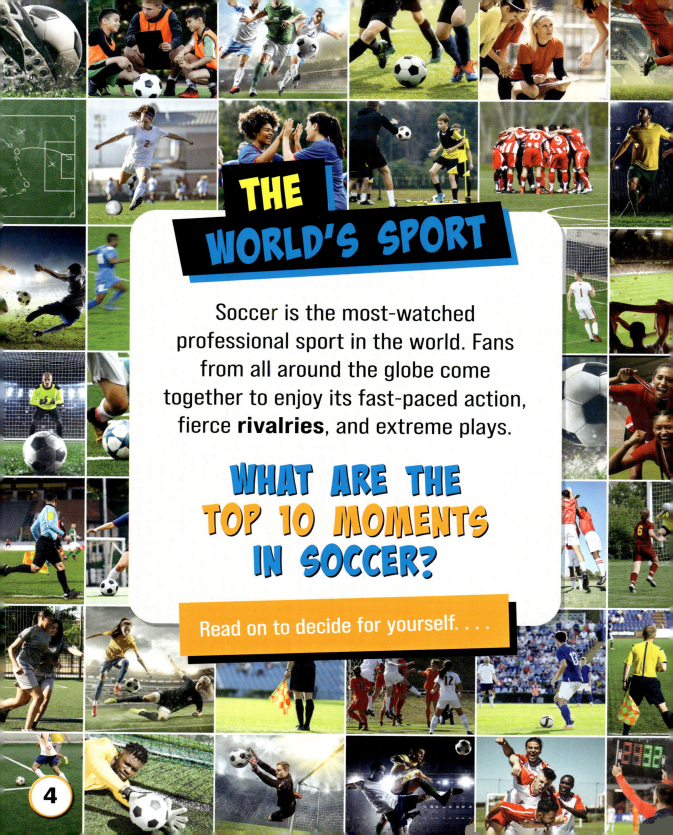

#10 RAPINOE'S OLIMPICO

August 6, 2012 ▪ Old Trafford ▪ Manchester, England

The **Olimpico** is one of soccer's most difficult—and impressive—plays. Despite its name, it took years for a player to score an Olimpico during the Olympics! The streak was broken when United States **forward** Megan Rapinoe took a corner kick during the 2012 semifinal against Canada. The ball made it just past the goalpost before hooking in to score!

Players watch as Rapinoe's ball goes in.

This goal became a key play in the 4–3 victory for the United States.

Rapinoe is the only player in Olympic history to score an Olimpico. She did it again in 2020!

#9 THE MIRACLE OF ISTANBUL

May 25, 2005 ▪ Atatürk Olympic Stadium ▪ Istanbul, Turkey

Going into halftime of the 2005 Union of European Football Associations (UEFA) Champions League final, Liverpool trailed Milan 3–0. After the break, Liverpool scored three goals in six minutes! Then, with the score tied, the match headed into extra time. A **penalty shootout** was needed to decide the winner. Liverpool won the shootout 3–2, completing a once-in-a-lifetime comeback!

The victory was Liverpool's fifth win in the tournament.

#8 GOING UNDEFEATED

July 8, 2014 • Estádio Mineirão • Belo Horizonte, Brazil

Both Germany and Brazil were undefeated entering the 2014 World Cup semifinals. Many fans expected a close game. Instead, Germany crushed Brazil! In the first half, Germany scored four goals in just six minutes. The team did not allow a single goal until the final minute. Germany's 7–1 victory was one of the most dominating performances in World Cup history.

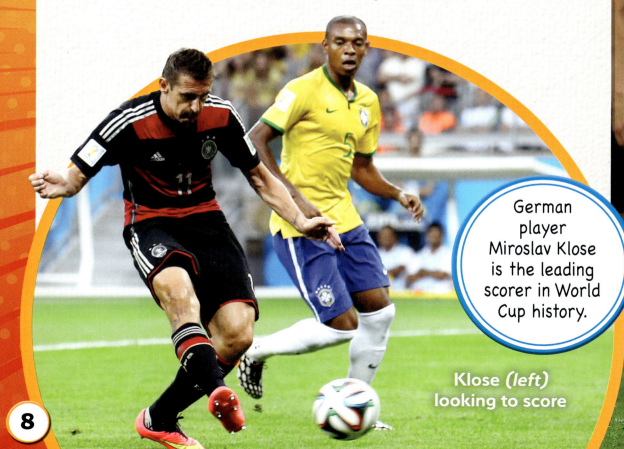

German player Miroslav Klose is the leading scorer in World Cup history.

Klose *(left)* looking to score

#7 THE HEADER HEARD 'ROUND THE WORLD

July 10, 2011 • Rudolf-Harbig-Stadion • Dresden, Germany

During the 2011 Women's World Cup quarterfinals, the United States trailed Brazil 2–1. Brazil caused a **turnover** with only seconds left. United States player Megan Rapinoe then launched the ball across the field. Her teammate Abby Wambach leapt in the air to score with a **header**! The play forced a penalty shootout that the United States won.

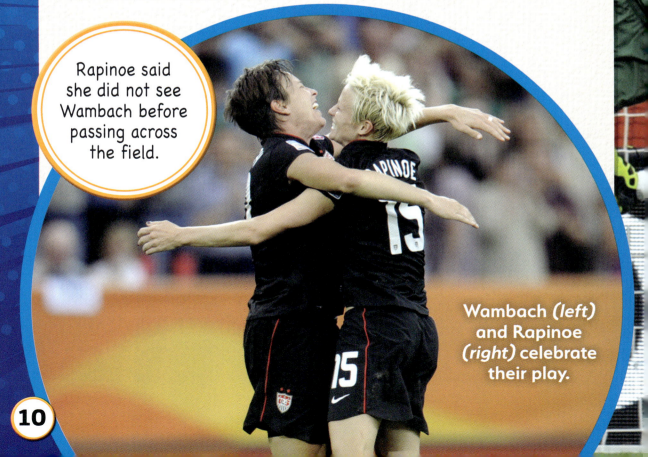

Rapinoe said she did not see Wambach before passing across the field.

Wambach *(left)* and Rapinoe *(right)* celebrate their play.

The United States went on to reach the 2011 World Cup finals.

Wambach is the all-time leading scorer in U.S. women's soccer.

Wambach (#20) makes a header goal.

Wambach's goal came in the match's 122nd minute!

#6 MESSI'S SOLO GOAL

April 18, 2007 • Camp Nou • Barcelona, Spain

Barcelona's Lionel Messi made an unstoppable solo goal during a 2007 **Copa del Rey** match against Getafe. Messi received the ball 60 yards (55 m) from Getafe's goal. He dodged two defenders, even kicking the ball between the legs of one before recovering it! Messi sped 30 yds. (27 m) down the field, passing three more defenders to score.

Messi would go on to score 672 goals for Barcelona—the most in team history.

At the time of the game, Messi was only 19 years old.

Messi has won more trophies than any other player in professional soccer.

#5 SAVING THE DAY

May 13, 2012 ▪ Etihad Stadium ▪ Manchester, England

During the final match of the 2011–2012 **Premier League** season, Manchester City and the Queens Park Rangers were tied. With 90 seconds of **stoppage time** left, Manchester City player Sergio Agüero fielded the ball. He sidestepped multiple Queens Park defenders to score one of the most famous goals in Premier League history! Manchester City won 3–2.

This win gave Manchester City their first Premier League title since 1968.

Agüero is the top scorer in Manchester City history.

Manchester City went on to win 7 more league titles over the next 12 years.

13

#4 KICKING FOR GOLD

August 20, 2016 • Maracanã Stadium • Rio de Janeiro, Brazil

Brazil took on Germany in the 2016 Olympic finals. With a 1–1 tie, the game was sent to a penalty shootout. Each team scored their first four penalty kicks. Brazil goalie Weverton blocked Germany's fifth attempt. Then, with the match on the line, Brazil player Neymar made the gold-winning score in front of the home crowd!

Neymar is the all-time leading scorer for Brazil.

Germany's goal during this game was the only one Brazil allowed during the entire 2016 Olympics.

Olympic gold was the last major soccer title that Brazil had yet to win.

The win gave Brazil their first Olympic gold medal in soccer.

#3 2022 WORLD CUP FINAL

December 18, 2022 • Lusail Stadium • Lusail, Qatar

Argentina entered the second half of the 2022 World Cup final against France with a 2–0 lead. France's forward Kylian Mbappé then scored twice in the final minutes, forcing extra time. After that, Mbappé and Argentina forward Lionel Messi each scored. This sent the game into a penalty shootout that led Argentina to their third World Cup victory!

This was Argentina's first World Cup win since 1986.

This game is considered one of the greatest of all time in soccer history.

Messi on the ground after scoring a goal during extra time

Mbappé became the second player in history to score a **hat trick** in a World Cup final.

With about 1.5 billion viewers, this match became one of the most-watched sporting events ever.

This was only the third time a World Cup was decided by a penalty shootout.

#2 PELÉ BURSTS ONTO THE SCENE

June 29, 1958 ▪ Råsunda Stadium ▪ Stockholm, Sweden

The 1958 World Cup introduced the world to Brazil's 17-year-old forward Pelé. Many considered him to be the greatest soccer player of all time. During Brazil's semifinal win against France, Pelé scored a hat trick. He then scored two more goals in Brazil's championship victory against Sweden. Pelé's performance helped Brazil win its first of five World Cups.

Pelé *(#10)* celebrates with his teammates.

Pelé would go on to win three World Cups—the most of any player in history.

The match between Sweden and Brazil had the most goals ever scored in a World Cup final.

Pelé is the youngest player to score a World Cup goal.

Pelé raises his hands after scoring during the 1958 World Cup final.

Pelé's real name was Edson Arantes do Nascimento.

Brazil has won more World Cups than any other country.

#1 THE GOAL OF THE CENTURY

June 22, 1986 ▪ Estadio Azteca ▪ Mexico City, Mexico

Argentina and England were scoreless 51 minutes into the 1986 World Cup quarterfinal. Then, Argentina player Diego Maradona scored twice in four minutes! The second time, he guided the ball himself more than halfway down the field. Maradona zigzagged past five England players to kick one of the most extreme solo goals in history! Argentina won 2–1.

Argentina went on to win the 1986 World Cup final against West Germany.

EVEN MORE EXTREME SOCCER MOMENTS

There are many professional soccer leagues around the world. Together, their teams have made lots of thrilling plays. Here are some other exciting top moments in soccer history.

1996 OLYMPICS
The 1996 Olympics was the first to include women's soccer. The United States team won the gold-medal game against China 2–1 on home turf.

VAN BASTEN'S VOLLEY
Netherlands player Arnold Mühren made a **cross** during 1988's UEFA Euro Final. The ball connected mid-air with teammate Marco van Basten, who scored a **volley** goal!

THE LAST-MINUTE GOAL
During the 2014 UEFA Champions League final, Real Madrid trailed Atlético 1–0. With time running out, Madrid's Sergio Ramos tied the game with a header!

GLOSSARY

Copa del Rey a yearly tournament played between Spain's soccer teams

cross a pass across the field to the area in front of an opponent's goal

forward an offensive player who is mostly responsible for scoring for their team

hat trick when a player scores three goals in one match

header when a player uses their head to control the ball

Olimpico a goal scored directly from a corner kick

penalty shootout a tie-breaking activity in soccer where each team takes turns kicking at the other's goal

Premier League the highest-level soccer league in England

rivalries strong competitions between two teams over a long period of time

stoppage time extra time added after each half of a soccer match to make up for time lost during the game

turnover a play where the offense accidentally loses possession of the ball

volley a powerful mid-air kick made before a pass can hit the ground

23

INDEX

defenders 12–13
forward 5, 16, 18
goalies 7, 14
kicking 5, 12, 14, 20
medals 5, 15, 22
penalties 6, 10, 14, 16–17
players 5, 8, 10, 12–14, 17–20, 22
quarterfinals 10, 20
scorers 8, 11, 13–14
semifinals 5, 8–9, 18
teammates 10, 18, 22
World Cup 8–11, 16–21

READ MORE

Braun, Eric. *Goal: The Science Behind Soccer's Most Exciting Plays (Sports Illustrated Kids: Science Behind the Plays).* North Mankato, MN: Capstone Press, 2025.

Hunter, Nick. *The Story of Soccer (Sports Illustrated Kids: Soccer Zone!).* North Mankato, MN: Capstone Press, 2025.

Streeter, Anthony. *World Cup All-Time Greats (All-Time Greats of Sports Championships).* Mendota Heights, MN: Press Box Books, 2025.

LEARN MORE ONLINE

1. Go to **FactSurfer.com** or scan the QR code below.
2. Enter "**10 Soccer Moments**" into the search box.
3. Click on the cover of this book to see a list of websites.

ABOUT THE AUTHOR

Nathan Sommer graduated from the University of Minnesota with degrees in journalism and political science. He lives in Minneapolis, Minnesota, and enjoys camping, hiking, and writing in his free time.